UNDERSTANDING

NARCISSISM

Unlocking The Complex

Layer Of Narcissism

MELISSA J. POWELL

TABLE OF CONTENT

15. Additional Resources

- Books, Articles, and Support Groups

INTRODUCTION

Narcissism, a term rooted in Greek mythology, has evolved into a complex psychological concept that continues to intrigue and puzzle researchers, clinicians, and individuals alike. In its simplest form, narcissism refers to a personality trait characterized by an excessive preoccupation with oneself, a profound need for admiration, and a lack of empathy for others. However, understanding narcissism goes far beyond these surface-level traits. It delves into the intricate web of emotions, behaviors, and motivations that shape the lives of those who possess narcissistic tendencies and those who interact with them. In this exploration, we will delve into the multifaceted world of narcissism, shedding light on its various dimensions, its origins, and its impact on individuals and society. By gaining a deeper comprehension of narcissism, we can hope to navigate its complexities more effectively, both in our personal lives and within the broader context of human behavior and relationships.

CHAPTER 1

Introduction

- Defining Narcissism

- The Importance of Understanding Narcissism

Introduction

Narcissism is a term that has permeated our cultural discourse, often used to describe individuals who exhibit self-centered and egotistical behavior. However, the concept of narcissism extends far beyond mere vanity or self-absorption. It encompasses a complex psychological construct with various facets, and its study holds significant importance in understanding human behavior and mental health. In this exploration, we will delve into the definition of narcissism, unravel its multifaceted nature, and underscore the vital importance of comprehending narcissism in today's society.

Defining Narcissism

Narcissism, as a concept, traces its origins to Greek mythology, where Narcissus, a beautiful youth, falls in love with his own reflection in a pool of water and eventually perishes as a result of his obsession. In the psychological context, the term was first introduced by Sigmund Freud, who used it to describe a developmental stage where an individual is excessively self-absorbed and lacks empathy for others. However, it was later popularized by Otto Rank, who explored narcissism as a fundamental aspect of human personality.

In contemporary psychology, narcissism is often defined as a personality trait characterized by a pervasive pattern of grandiosity, an insatiable need for admiration, and a lack of empathy for others. Psychologists commonly distinguish between two main types of narcissism: grandiose narcissism and vulnerable narcissism.

1. Grandiose Narcissism: Individuals with grandiose narcissism exhibit an inflated sense of self-importance, a preoccupation with fantasies of success and power, and a constant need for external validation. They often display arrogance and a disregard for the feelings and needs of others.

2. Vulnerable Narcissism: Vulnerable narcissists, on the other hand, display a more fragile and defensive form of narcissism. They are hypersensitive to criticism, have a constant fear of rejection, and often suffer from low self-esteem beneath their outwardly confident facade.

It is crucial to note that narcissism exists on a spectrum, and not all narcissistic traits are necessarily harmful. Some level of narcissism is considered a normal and healthy aspect of human development, as it can contribute to self-confidence and resilience. However, when narcissistic traits become extreme and pervasive, they can lead to significant interpersonal and psychological problems.

The Importance of Understanding Narcissism

Understanding narcissism is of paramount importance in several domains, ranging from personal relationships to mental health and even societal dynamics. Here, we outline the key reasons why comprehending narcissism is so crucial:

1. Relationship Dynamics: Narcissistic individuals often struggle with forming and maintaining healthy relationships. Their excessive self-centeredness and lack of empathy can lead to conflicts, emotional abuse, and manipulation within relationships. By recognizing narcissistic traits, individuals can better navigate and protect themselves from toxic interactions.

2. Mental Health: Narcissistic Personality Disorder (NPD) is a diagnosable mental health condition associated with extreme narcissism. Understanding the nature of narcissism is essential for mental health professionals in diagnosing and treating NPD effectively. Moreover, individuals with narcissistic traits may benefit from therapy and interventions to improve their interpersonal skills and overall well-being.

3. Workplace Environments: Narcissistic traits can be observed in the workplace, where individuals with grandiose narcissism may seek power and control at the expense of their colleagues. Recognizing narcissistic behavior in professional settings can help organizations manage conflicts, maintain a healthy work environment, and promote effective leadership.

4. Social Media and Celebrity Culture: The rise of social media has amplified narcissistic tendencies in many individuals.

Understanding the influence of narcissism on social media usage and its impact on mental health is crucial in a digitally connected world. Moreover, celebrity culture often celebrates narcissistic traits, making it essential to critically evaluate the role of fame and admiration in our society.

5. Parenting and Child Development: Parents' narcissistic tendencies can have a profound impact on their children's upbringing. Recognizing the signs of narcissism in parenting can help protect children from emotional neglect and abuse, promoting healthier development.

6. Cultural and Societal Trends: Narcissism is not limited to individual behaviors; it can manifest on a broader societal level. Analyzing the prevalence of narcissistic traits in society can shed light on cultural trends, such as consumerism, materialism, and the pursuit of fame, which may influence collective values and priorities.

In conclusion, narcissism is a multifaceted psychological construct that plays a significant role in various aspects of our lives. It is not merely a matter of vanity or self-absorption but a complex trait with far-reaching implications. Recognizing and understanding narcissism is essential for fostering healthy relationships, promoting mental well-being, and navigating the challenges of our interconnected world. As we delve deeper into this exploration, we will uncover the intricate dimensions of narcissism and its profound impact on individuals and society.

CHAPTER 2

Historical Perspectives

- The Myth of Narcissus

- Early Psychological Concepts

The Myth of Narcissus:

The story of Narcissus originates from Greek mythology, a rich source of narratives that often serve as allegorical tales with profound psychological and philosophical implications. The tale of Narcissus is no exception, as it explores themes of self-love, beauty, and the consequences of excessive self-absorption.

In the most popular version of the myth, Narcissus is described as a young and exceptionally handsome youth. His beauty was so captivating that it drew the attention of both men and women, but Narcissus remained indifferent to their advances. His heart remained untouched by the love of others, leading to a sense of isolation and emotional emptiness.

The pivotal moment in the myth occurs when Narcissus encounters his own reflection in a pool of water. Gazing at his own image, he becomes utterly infatuated with it, unable to tear himself away. His obsession with his own reflection consumes him, ultimately leading to his demise as he pines away by the pool, unable to reach the object of his desire.

The myth of Narcissus, though ancient, presents a timeless portrayal of the human condition. It serves as a cautionary tale, warning against the dangers of excessive self-love and preoccupation with one's own image and desires. Narcissus's fate serves as a stark reminder that unchecked self-absorption can lead to spiritual and emotional isolation, preventing meaningful connections with others.

Early Psychological Concepts:

The myth of Narcissus has had a profound influence on early psychological concepts, particularly within the realm of psychoanalysis and the study of narcissism. Here, we will explore how this myth has shaped the understanding of human behavior and the development of psychological theories.

1. Freudian Interpretation: Sigmund Freud, the father of psychoanalysis, drew upon the myth of Narcissus to develop his theory of narcissism. Freud distinguished between primary narcissism, which is a natural self-love inherent in every

individual, and secondary narcissism, which arises from an excessive fixation on the self. He argued that an imbalance between these two forms of narcissism could lead to various psychological disorders. Freud's work laid the foundation for the study of narcissistic personality traits and disorders.

2. Kohut's Self-Psychology: Heinz Kohut, a prominent psychoanalyst, expanded on Freud's ideas by developing self-psychology. Kohut emphasized the importance of a healthy narcissistic development in early childhood. He argued that narcissism plays a crucial role in forming a stable sense of self and healthy interpersonal relationships. Kohut's work highlighted the positive aspects of narcissism, challenging the notion that it is solely pathological.

3. Object Relations Theory: Object relations theorists, such as Melanie Klein and Ronald Fairbairn, explored how early relationships with caregivers shape an individual's self-concept. They viewed narcissism as a necessary phase of development, where the infant's primary focus is on satisfying their own needs. These early experiences influence one's capacity for intimacy and empathy later in life, shedding light on the complex interplay between self-love and love for others.

4. Modern Perspectives: Today, narcissism remains a subject of intense study within psychology. The narcissistic personality disorder (NPD) is recognized in the Diagnostic and Statistical Manual of Mental Disorders (DSM-5), reflecting the enduring relevance of narcissism as a psychological construct. Researchers

continue to investigate the origins, manifestations, and treatment of narcissistic traits and NPD.

In conclusion, the myth of Narcissus has left an indelible mark on the study of human behavior and psychology. It serves as a timeless cautionary tale, reminding us of the potential consequences of excessive self-absorption. From Freud's pioneering work to modern research on narcissism, the myth continues to inspire and inform our understanding of the intricate relationship between self-love, identity, and interpersonal dynamics in the complex tapestry of the human psyche.

CHAPTER 3

Types of Narcissism

- Grandiose Narcissism

- Vulnerable Narcissism

- Covert Narcissism

Narcissism is a complex personality trait characterized by excessive self-love, a need for admiration, and a lack of empathy for others. While narcissism exists on a spectrum, researchers have identified different types that help us understand the nuances of this trait. The three primary types of narcissism are Grandiose Narcissism, Vulnerable Narcissism, and Covert Narcissism. Each type exhibits distinct behaviors and underlying psychological mechanisms.

1. Grandiose Narcissism:

Grandiose Narcissism is perhaps the most well-known and stereotypical form of narcissism. Individuals with this type tend to exhibit the following traits:

- Exaggerated Self-Importance: Grandiose narcissists have an inflated sense of self-worth. They believe they are superior to others in various aspects, such as intelligence, attractiveness, or achievements.

- Need for Admiration: They constantly seek admiration and validation from others. They thrive on attention, praise, and recognition.

- Lack of Empathy: Grandiose narcissists often struggle to empathize with the emotions and needs of others. They may disregard or belittle the feelings of those around them.

- Manipulative Behavior: They can be manipulative and exploit others to achieve their goals. They may use charm and charisma to manipulate people into serving their interests.

- Risk-Taking and Impulsivity: Grandiose narcissists may engage in risky behaviors, as they believe they are immune to negative consequences. They often act impulsively without considering the potential harm.

- Fragile Self-Esteem: Paradoxically, their self-esteem is quite fragile, leading them to react strongly to criticism or perceived threats to their self-image.

2. Vulnerable Narcissism:

Vulnerable Narcissism, also known as Fragile Narcissism, presents a contrasting face to grandiose narcissism. Individuals with this type display the following characteristics:

- Low Self-Esteem: Unlike grandiose narcissists, those with vulnerable narcissism have underlying feelings of inadequacy and self-doubt. They mask these feelings with defensive behaviors.

- Hypersensitivity to Criticism: Vulnerable narcissists are extremely sensitive to criticism or perceived rejection. They may react with anger, withdrawal, or even depression when faced with negative feedback.

- Avoidance of Risk: They tend to avoid taking risks and avoid situations where they might face failure or humiliation.

- Fantasy of Success: They may have grandiose fantasies about success, but these fantasies often remain unfulfilled due to their fear of failure.

- Depression and Anxiety: Vulnerable narcissists are more prone to experiencing symptoms of depression and anxiety. Their internal turmoil can lead to mood swings and emotional instability.

- Passive-Aggressive Behavior: They may employ passive-aggressive tactics to deal with their insecurities, such as giving others the silent treatment or engaging in indirect forms of aggression.

3. Covert Narcissism:

Covert Narcissism is a less obvious form of narcissism, making it challenging to identify. People with covert narcissism exhibit the following characteristics:

- Inwardly Focused: Covert narcissists are preoccupied with their own emotions, thoughts, and desires. They may appear introverted or shy.

- Need for Special Treatment: They believe they are unique or special and expect others to recognize and cater to their needs without explicitly expressing them.

- Manipulative Victimhood: Covert narcissists often adopt a victim mentality. They may use passive-aggressive tactics to manipulate others into fulfilling their desires.

- Low Self-Esteem: Similar to vulnerable narcissism, covert narcissists harbor feelings of inadequacy but cover them up with a façade of modesty.

- Difficulty Forming Genuine Relationships: They may struggle to establish deep, meaningful connections with others because their self-centeredness hinders true emotional intimacy.

- Secretive Behavior: Covert narcissists tend to be secretive about their true feelings and motives, making it challenging for others to understand their underlying intentions.

Understanding these different types of narcissism can be valuable for both individuals dealing with narcissistic traits and those interacting with narcissistic individuals. Recognizing the type of narcissism at play can help in determining appropriate strategies

CHAPTER 4

Narcissistic Personality Disorder (NPD)

- Diagnostic Criteria

- Common Traits and Behaviors

- Prevalence Rates

Narcissistic Personality Disorder (NPD) is a complex and challenging mental health condition that affects individuals in various aspects of their lives. This personality disorder is characterized by a pervasive pattern of grandiosity, a need for admiration, and a lack of empathy. In this comprehensive discussion, we will delve into the diagnostic criteria, common traits and behaviors, and prevalence rates of NPD, shedding light on this complex condition.

Diagnostic Criteria:

To receive a diagnosis of Narcissistic Personality Disorder, an individual must exhibit a persistent pattern of the following criteria, as outlined in the Diagnostic and Statistical Manual of Mental Disorders, Fifth Edition (DSM-5):

1. Grandiose Sense of Self-Importance: People with NPD often exaggerate their achievements and talents, expecting to be recognized as superior without commensurate achievements.

2. Fantasies of Success, Power, Beauty, or Ideal Love: They have a preoccupation with fantasies of unlimited success, power, brilliance, beauty, or ideal love.

3. Belief in Own Uniqueness: Individuals with NPD believe that they are unique and can only be understood by, or should associate with, other high-status or special individuals.

4. Need for Excessive Admiration: They require excessive admiration and regularly seek it from others, often relying on others for self-esteem regulation.

5. **Sense of Entitlement:** People with NPD often have a sense of entitlement and expect special treatment and unquestioning compliance with their expectations.

6. Interpersonally Exploitative Behavior: They frequently exploit others for their own gain and lack empathy for the feelings and needs of others.

7. Lack of Empathy: A hallmark trait of NPD is a profound lack of empathy, an inability to recognize or identify with the feelings and needs of others.

8. Envy of Others or Belief That Others Are Envious: Individuals with NPD are often envious of others or believe that others are envious of them.

9. Arrogance and Haughtiness: They display arrogant, haughty behaviors and attitudes.

Common Traits and Behaviors:

Beyond the diagnostic criteria, there are several common traits and behaviors associated with NPD:

1. Manipulative Behavior: People with NPD can be highly manipulative, using others to achieve their own goals without regard for the consequences.

2. Inflated Self-Image: They maintain an inflated self-image, often exaggerating their talents and achievements, even when the reality does not support such claims.

3. Fragile Self-Esteem: Paradoxically, underneath the grandiose exterior, individuals with NPD often have fragile self-esteem, which is easily wounded by criticism or perceived slights.

4. Difficulty in Maintaining Relationships: NPD can lead to difficulty in maintaining healthy relationships, as their need for admiration and lack of empathy can strain interpersonal connections.

5. Work and Career Implications: While some with NPD may excel in their careers due to their confidence and ambition, their interpersonal difficulties can lead to problems in the workplace.

6. Emotional Regulation Challenges: They may struggle with regulating their emotions, especially in response to perceived criticism or rejection.

7. Relationship Patterns: People with NPD may have a pattern of idealizing others initially, then devaluing them once they no longer serve their needs.

Prevalence Rates:

Estimating the exact prevalence of Narcissistic Personality Disorder is challenging due to various factors, including underreporting and the complex nature of the condition. However, research suggests that NPD is not as common as some other personality disorders.

According to the DSM-5, the estimated prevalence of NPD in the general population is around 0.5% to 1%. However, the prevalence rate may vary among different populations and age groups. It's important to note that narcissistic traits, which exist on a spectrum, are more prevalent than the full-blown disorder itself.

NPD appears to be more common in men than in women, though some experts argue that this gender difference may be due to underdiagnosis in women or differences in how the disorder manifests.

In conclusion, Narcissistic Personality Disorder is a complex condition characterized by grandiosity, a need for admiration, and a lack of empathy. Understanding its diagnostic criteria, common traits and behaviors, and prevalence rates is crucial for recognizing and addressing this challenging mental health issue. While NPD is relatively rare, its impact on individuals and those around them can be profound, highlighting the importance of early diagnosis and appropriate treatment.

CHAPTER 5

Developmental Roots

- Childhood Influences

- Nature vs. Nurture Debate

The study of human development has long fascinated scholars, scientists, and psychologists. It seeks to unravel the intricate processes by which individuals grow, learn, and evolve over their lifespan. At the heart of this exploration lie two fundamental concepts: childhood influences and the nature vs. nurture debate. These concepts not only shape our understanding of human development but also guide our approach to parenting, education, and societal policies.

Childhood Influences

Childhood is a critical phase in human development, characterized by rapid physical, cognitive, and emotional changes. It is during this period that the foundation for an individual's personality, values, and behavior is laid. Childhood influences can be categorized into several key factors:

1. Family Environment:

The family is often considered the primary socialization agent in a child's life. Parenting styles, family dynamics, and the quality of relationships within the family can profoundly impact a child's development. For instance, a nurturing and supportive family environment can foster a child's self-esteem and emotional well-being, while a dysfunctional family can lead to various psychological issues.

2. Peer Relationships:

As children grow, they begin to interact more with their peers. These interactions play a crucial role in shaping social skills, values, and even interests. Positive peer relationships can promote healthy development, while negative peer experiences may lead to social challenges and emotional difficulties.

3. Education and Schooling:

Formal education is a significant aspect of childhood. The quality of education, teaching methods, and school environment can have a profound impact on a child's intellectual and academic development. Early educational experiences can shape a child's attitudes toward learning and influence their future career choices.

4. Socioeconomic Status:

The socioeconomic status of a child's family can influence their access to resources, opportunities, and experiences. Children from economically disadvantaged backgrounds may face obstacles that hinder their development, while those from more privileged backgrounds may have greater advantages.

5. Culture and Ethnicity:

Cultural factors, including traditions, beliefs, and values, can shape a child's identity and worldview. Children raised in diverse cultural environments may develop a broader perspective and adaptability, while those from more homogeneous backgrounds may have a stronger connection to their cultural heritage.

The Nature vs. Nurture Debate

The nature vs. nurture debate is a long-standing and complex discussion in the field of psychology and human development. It revolves around the question of whether genetics (nature) or environmental factors (nurture) have a more significant influence on an individual's traits, behaviors, and development. While the debate is ongoing, it is widely accepted that both nature and nurture interact to shape human development.

1. Nature (Genetics):

Genetic factors play a crucial role in determining various aspects of human development, such as physical traits, intelligence, and predisposition to certain health conditions. For example, genes can influence a person's height, eye color, and susceptibility to diseases.

2. Nurture (Environment):

Environmental factors encompass everything outside of genetics, including family, culture, education, and experiences. These factors interact with an individual's genetic predispositions to influence development. For instance, a genetically gifted athlete may only reach their full potential with the right training and opportunities.

3. Interactionist Perspective:

Contemporary researchers emphasize the interaction between nature and nurture. This perspective acknowledges that genes and the environment are interdependent, with one influencing the other. For instance, a child's genetic predisposition for musical talent may only manifest if they are exposed to music education and practice.

4. Epigenetics:

Epigenetics is a fascinating field that explores how environmental factors can alter gene expression. It suggests that experiences and exposures during childhood can leave lasting marks on an individual's genetic code, affecting their health and development.

Conclusion

Understanding developmental roots, including childhood influences and the nature vs. nurture debate, is essential for comprehending human growth and behavior. While childhood influences set the stage for development, the nature vs. nurture debate reminds us that both genetic and environmental factors are intricately intertwined in shaping who we become. Recognizing this complexity can inform parenting practices, educational strategies, and policies aimed at supporting healthy development and maximizing human potential. As we continue to explore these concepts, we gain deeper insights into the rich tapestry of human development and the myriad factors that contribute to our unique individuality.

CHAPTER 6

Spotting Narcissism

- Red Flags and Warning Signs

- Contrasting Healthy Self-Esteem

Narcissism is a term that has gained significant attention in recent years, both in psychological circles and everyday discourse. While a certain level of self-confidence and self-love is healthy and necessary for personal growth, narcissism represents an extreme end of the self-esteem spectrum. In this article, we will explore how to spot narcissism by examining the red flags and warning signs. Additionally, we will contrast narcissistic behavior with healthy self-esteem to provide a comprehensive understanding of this complex issue.

Spotting Narcissism: Red Flags and Warning Signs

1. Excessive Self-Centeredness: One of the most noticeable red flags of narcissism is an excessive focus on oneself. Narcissists often monopolize conversations, redirect discussions to be about them, and show little interest in others' experiences or feelings.

2. Lack of Empathy: Narcissists struggle to empathize with others. They may dismiss or downplay others' emotions and are often insensitive to the needs and feelings of those around them.

3. Grandiose Sense of Self-Importance: Narcissists have an inflated view of themselves. They often believe they are unique, exceptional, or entitled to special treatment. This grandiosity can manifest in boasting, bragging, or exaggerating their achievements.

4. Manipulative Behavior: Narcissists can be highly manipulative, using charm and charisma to get what they want. They may exploit others emotionally, financially, or psychologically without guilt or remorse.

5. Constant Need for Validation: Narcissists require constant validation and admiration from others to maintain their self-esteem. They often fish for compliments and become deeply distressed if they feel ignored or criticized.

6. Difficulty Accepting Criticism: Narcissists have a fragile self-esteem that cannot withstand criticism. They react defensively, become angry, or may even seek revenge when their flaws or mistakes are pointed out.

7. Unrealistic Expectations of Favoritism: Narcissists expect preferential treatment and often believe they deserve special privileges, even when such expectations are unwarranted.

8. Shallow Relationships: While narcissists may have many acquaintances, their relationships tend to be shallow and transactional. They often struggle to form deep, meaningful connections.

9. Envy and Jealousy: Narcissists may be envious of others' success and often engage in competitive behavior to outshine or undermine those they perceive as threats.

10. Frequent Boundary Violations: They frequently disregard personal boundaries, invading others' personal space or privacy without hesitation.

Contrasting Healthy Self-Esteem

Now that we've examined the red flags of narcissism, let's contrast them with indicators of healthy self-esteem:

1. Self-Confidence vs. Arrogance: Healthy self-esteem involves self-confidence without arrogance. Confident individuals acknowledge their abilities without belittling others.

2. Empathy and Compassion: People with healthy self-esteem can empathize with others' emotions and offer support without expecting constant praise.

3. Realistic Self-Appraisal: They have a balanced view of their strengths and weaknesses and can accept constructive criticism.

4. Respect for Boundaries: Individuals with healthy self-esteem respect personal boundaries and seek consent before engaging in any interactions.

5. Interdependence: They understand the value of mutually beneficial relationships and cooperation, fostering deeper connections with others.

6. Emotional Resilience: Healthy self-esteem allows individuals to handle criticism and setbacks without becoming defensive or resorting to manipulation.

7. Validation from Within: They derive their self-worth from internal sources rather than relying solely on external validation.

8. Admiration vs. Need for Worship: While healthy individuals appreciate admiration, they do not require constant adoration to maintain their self-esteem.

Conclusion

Spotting narcissism is crucial for maintaining healthy relationships and understanding the dynamics of personal interactions. By recognizing the red flags and warning signs, we can better navigate encounters with narcissistic individuals. Additionally, understanding the contrast between narcissistic behavior and healthy self-esteem helps us appreciate the importance of striking a balance between self-confidence and empathy in our own lives. Building healthy self-esteem and cultivating empathetic connections can lead to more fulfilling and harmonious relationships.

CHAPTER 7

Impact on Relationships

- Narcissism in Friendships

- Narcissism in Family Dynamics

- Narcissism in Romantic Relationships

Narcissism is a personality trait that has the potential to profoundly affect various aspects of our lives, including our relationships. It manifests as an excessive self-focus, a need for admiration, and a lack of empathy for others. While a certain degree of narcissism is normal and even healthy, when it becomes extreme, it can wreak havoc on the dynamics of friendships, family relationships, and romantic partnerships. In this essay, we will explore the impact of narcissism in each of these contexts, delving into the challenges it presents and potential strategies for dealing with them.

Narcissism in Friendships:

Friendships are often our first experiences of social bonding outside the family. They are built on trust, mutual support, and shared experiences. However, when one or more individuals in a friendship display narcissistic traits, these core elements of friendship can be compromised.

One of the most noticeable effects of narcissism in friendships is the imbalance in attention and validation. Narcissistic friends tend to dominate conversations, steering discussions toward their own achievements, concerns, and interests. This constant need for validation can be exhausting for their friends, who may feel that their own experiences and feelings are constantly overshadowed.

Moreover, narcissistic friends may have difficulty empathizing with their peers' struggles or celebrating their successes genuinely. Their lack of empathy can lead to emotional distance and a sense of being unheard or unsupported in the friendship.

To maintain a healthy friendship with a narcissistic individual, setting boundaries and promoting open communication is essential. Friends can gently assert their own needs and encourage their narcissistic friends to practice empathy and active listening. However, if the narcissism is extreme and detrimental to one's well-being, it may be necessary to reconsider the friendship.

Narcissism in Family Dynamics:

Narcissism within a family can have profound and long-lasting effects. When a parent or caregiver exhibits narcissistic traits, it can create a challenging environment for children to grow and develop. Such families often prioritize the narcissistic individual's needs and desires over those of others, including their own children.

Children raised in narcissistic households may struggle with low self-esteem, as they constantly receive the message that their needs and feelings are inconsequential. They may become people-pleasers or, conversely, develop their own narcissistic traits as a defense mechanism.

Siblings in such families can also experience strained relationships. The narcissistic parent may play favorites, causing jealousy and resentment among siblings. This can lead to lifelong conflicts and emotional scars.

Breaking free from the cycle of narcissism in the family often requires therapy and open communication. Children may need to establish boundaries with their narcissistic parents and seek support to heal from the emotional wounds of their upbringing. Siblings can benefit from therapy as well, to address their own issues and work towards healthier relationships.

Narcissism in Romantic Relationships:

Perhaps the most complex and emotionally charged context in which narcissism can wreak havoc is romantic relationships. At the beginning of a relationship, the charm, confidence, and charisma often associated with narcissism can be alluring. However, as the relationship progresses, the challenges become more apparent.

Narcissistic partners tend to view their significant other as an extension of themselves, rather than as an independent individual. They may become controlling and possessive, seeking constant affirmation of their desirability and importance. This can stifle the autonomy and self-esteem of their partners.

Furthermore, conflicts in such relationships can be particularly challenging. Narcissistic individuals may refuse to accept responsibility for their actions, deflecting blame onto their partners. This pattern of behavior can erode trust and create a hostile atmosphere within the relationship.

Surviving and thriving in a relationship with a narcissist requires immense patience, understanding, and often professional help. Couples therapy can provide a safe space for communication and conflict resolution. However, it's important to recognize that not all narcissistic individuals are willing to change, and in some cases, leaving the relationship may be the healthiest choice.

In conclusion, narcissism can have a profound impact on relationships in various contexts. Whether it's in friendships, family dynamics, or romantic partnerships, the excessive self-focus and lack of empathy associated with narcissism can create challenges and emotional turmoil. While it is possible to navigate these relationships with care, setting boundaries, and seeking professional guidance, it is also important to prioritize one's own well-being and consider the possibility of distancing oneself from toxic relationships when necessary. Ultimately, nurturing healthy and balanced relationships is essential for our emotional and psychological well-being.

CHAPTER 8

Psychological Mechanisms

- Ego Defense Mechanisms

- Cognitive Biases

Psychological mechanisms play a crucial role in shaping our thoughts, behaviors, and emotions. They are the hidden gears of our mind, influencing how we perceive the world and how we cope with it. In this exploration, we will delve into two fundamental psychological mechanisms: Ego Defense Mechanisms and Cognitive Biases. These mechanisms shed light on how our minds protect us from distressing thoughts and influence our decision-making processes.

I. Ego Defense Mechanisms

1. The Ego and Its Role

Sigmund Freud introduced the concept of the ego as a central component of the human psyche. The ego is the conscious part of our mind responsible for mediating between the desires of the id (our primitive instincts) and the constraints of the superego (our moral and societal norms). To maintain psychological equilibrium, the ego employs various defense mechanisms when it faces internal or external threats.

2. Repression

Repression is perhaps the most fundamental ego defense mechanism. It involves pushing distressing thoughts, memories, or emotions into the unconscious mind. This mechanism allows us to temporarily forget or block out painful experiences, protecting our mental well-being. However, repressed material can resurface in unexpected ways, potentially leading to psychological issues.

3. Denial

Denial is the refusal to accept reality or acknowledge the existence of something distressing. It serves as a protective shield against overwhelming emotions or facts that challenge one's self-concept. For example, someone diagnosed with a terminal illness may initially deny the diagnosis to maintain a sense of control and hope.

4. Projection

Projection involves attributing one's own undesirable thoughts, feelings, or traits to others. By projecting negative aspects of themselves onto someone else, individuals can avoid acknowledging these aspects within themselves. This mechanism can lead to misinterpretations and conflicts in interpersonal relationships.

5. Rationalization

Rationalization is a process of creating logical explanations or justifications for irrational behavior or thoughts. People use this mechanism to preserve their self-esteem and avoid guilt or shame. For instance, someone might rationalize cheating on a test by convincing themselves that everyone else does it.

6. Sublimation

Sublimation involves channeling unacceptable impulses or emotions into socially acceptable activities. Instead of acting on destructive desires, individuals redirect their energy into productive pursuits. An example is using intense competitive drive to excel in sports or career, channeling aggressive tendencies into healthy competition.

7. Displacement

Displacement involves transferring negative emotions or impulses from their original source onto a less threatening target. An individual who is angry at their boss but cannot express it may go home and take out their frustration on their family members or pets. This redirection helps protect the individual from the potential consequences of confronting the real issue.

8. Regression

Regression occurs when an individual reverts to childlike behaviors or coping mechanisms in times of stress. For example, an adult might start thumb-sucking or seeking excessive comfort when facing a traumatic event. This temporary retreat to a simpler, safer time can provide emotional relief.

9. Intellectualization

Intellectualization is a defense mechanism that involves approaching distressing situations or emotions with a detached, analytical mindset. By focusing on the intellectual aspects, individuals distance themselves from the emotional impact. This can hinder genuine emotional processing but offers a sense of control in challenging situations.

II. Cognitive Biases

1. Introduction to Cognitive Biases

Cognitive biases are systematic patterns of thinking that deviate from objective and rational judgment. They are a result of mental shortcuts and heuristics our brains use to process information efficiently. While these biases can be helpful in simplifying complex decision-making, they often lead to errors and irrational judgments.

2. Confirmation Bias

Confirmation bias is the tendency to seek out, interpret, and remember information that confirms preexisting beliefs while ignoring or dismissing contradictory evidence. This bias can reinforce stereotypes and hinder open-mindedness, making it difficult to change one's views.

3. Anchoring Bias

The anchoring bias occurs when individuals rely too heavily on the first piece of information encountered (the "anchor") when making decisions. Subsequent information is often interpreted in relation to this anchor, leading to skewed judgments. For example, in negotiations, the initial price suggested can heavily influence the final agreement.

4. Availability Heuristic

The availability heuristic involves estimating the probability of an event based on its availability in memory. If a recent event is vivid or memorable, it is more likely to be perceived as common or significant. This bias can lead to overestimating the likelihood of rare or dramatic events.

5. Hindsight Bias

Hindsight bias, also known as the "I knew it all along" effect, is the tendency to believe

CHAPTER 9

Treating Narcissism

- Therapeutic Approaches

- Challenges in Treatment

Narcissism, a personality trait characterized by excessive self-love, a grandiose sense of self-importance, and a lack of empathy, can have a profound impact on an individual's life and relationships. While narcissism exists on a spectrum, individuals with narcissistic personality disorder (NPD) often require therapeutic intervention to address their maladaptive behaviors and improve their quality of life. In this article, we will explore therapeutic approaches to treating narcissism and the challenges that therapists and individuals face in the process.

Therapeutic Approaches:

1. Psychotherapy:

Psychotherapy is the cornerstone of narcissism treatment. Several modalities have shown promise in helping individuals with narcissistic traits or NPD:

- Cognitive-Behavioral Therapy (CBT): CBT helps individuals recognize and challenge distorted thought patterns and behaviors associated with narcissism. It encourages self-reflection and empathy development.

- Dialectical Behavior Therapy (DBT): DBT combines cognitive and behavioral techniques to help individuals regulate their emotions and improve interpersonal skills. It can be particularly useful in managing impulsivity and emotional instability in narcissistic individuals.

- Psychodynamic Therapy: This approach explores the underlying causes of narcissism, often rooted in childhood experiences. By uncovering and addressing these deep-seated issues, individuals can gain insight into their behaviors and motivations.

2. Group Therapy:

Group therapy sessions provide narcissistic individuals with opportunities for social interaction and feedback. Interacting with peers can help them better understand how their behavior affects others and practice empathy and perspective-taking.

3. Mindfulness and Self-Compassion:

Mindfulness practices and self-compassion exercises can help individuals with narcissistic traits become more aware of their thoughts and emotions. These techniques promote self-reflection and reduce the need for constant external validation.

4. Medication:

While medication isn't a primary treatment for narcissism, it can be used to manage co-occurring conditions like depression or anxiety, which often accompany narcissistic personality disorder.

Challenges in Treatment:

1. Resistance to Change:

One of the primary challenges in treating narcissism is the individual's resistance to acknowledging their problematic behaviors. Narcissists often have a strong desire to maintain their grandiose self-image, making it difficult for them to accept criticism or engage in therapy.

2. Lack of Motivation for Change:

Many narcissistic individuals may not see a need for treatment because they believe they are superior or flawless. Convincing them to engage in therapy can be a daunting task.

3. Comorbidity:

Narcissism frequently co-occurs with other mental health issues, such as substance abuse, depression, or borderline personality disorder. Treating narcissism alongside these conditions can be complex and require a multifaceted approach.

4. Duration of Treatment:

Therapy for narcissism is often a long-term process. Significant changes in behavior and self-perception take time, and individuals may need ongoing support and therapy for an extended period.

5. Impact on Relationships:

Narcissistic behaviors can cause severe damage to relationships. Rebuilding trust and repairing these relationships can be challenging and time-consuming.

6. Identifying and Addressing Underlying Trauma:

For individuals with narcissistic traits stemming from childhood trauma, delving into these painful experiences can be emotionally difficult. Therapists must handle this delicately.

7. Relapse Risk:

Even after successful therapy, narcissistic individuals may be at risk of relapse, especially during times of stress or personal challenges. Ongoing self-awareness and support are crucial to preventing this.

In conclusion, treating narcissism is a complex and challenging endeavor that requires a multifaceted approach. Psychotherapy, group therapy, mindfulness, and medication can all play a role in helping individuals with narcissistic traits or NPD. However, therapists and individuals must navigate resistance to change, comorbidity, and the long-term nature of treatment. Ultimately, addressing narcissism can lead to healthier relationships and improved well-being, but it requires patience, persistence, and a commitment to self-reflection and personal growth.

CHAPTER 10

Narcissism in Popular Culture

- Narcissism in Literature and Film

- Celebrities and Narcissism

Narcissism has always been a pervasive and intriguing aspect of human psychology, and its presence in popular culture provides a mirror through which we can examine the values, trends, and anxieties of contemporary society. In this exploration, we delve into how narcissism is portrayed in literature and film, as well as its intertwining relationship with celebrities in the realm of popular culture.

Narcissism in Literature and Film

Narcissism, as a concept, takes its name from the Greek mythological figure Narcissus, who fell in love with his own reflection. This theme of self-obsession has been a recurring motif in literature and film for centuries. One of the most iconic literary representations of narcissism is F. Scott Fitzgerald's "The Great Gatsby." The novel revolves around Jay Gatsby, a self-made millionaire who is hopelessly infatuated with Daisy Buchanan. Gatsby's relentless pursuit of Daisy and his obsession with his own image as a wealthy and successful man exemplify narcissistic traits. The green light at the end of Daisy's dock, symbolizing

Gatsby's unattainable desires, reflects his narcissistic fixation on a fantasy.

Another classic example of narcissism in literature can be found in Oscar Wilde's "The Picture of Dorian Gray." The titular character, Dorian Gray, remains eternally youthful while his portrait ages and reflects the moral decay of his soul. Dorian's pursuit of eternal beauty and disregard for the consequences of his actions are emblematic of narcissistic tendencies. This novel raises essential questions about the price of vanity and the destructive nature of narcissism.

In the realm of film, David Fincher's "Fight Club" offers a darker and more subversive exploration of narcissism. The unnamed protagonist, played by Edward Norton, becomes entangled with Tyler Durden, played by Brad Pitt, who represents his darker, more liberated self. As the story unfolds, it becomes evident that Tyler Durden is a manifestation of the protagonist's narcissistic desires, embodying a reckless and destructive ego that ultimately leads to chaos.

These literary and cinematic examples highlight the multifaceted nature of narcissism, from the allure of wealth and beauty to the destructive consequences of unchecked self-obsession. They invite audiences to examine their own desires and the potential consequences of pursuing them to extremes.

Celebrities and Narcissism

In the age of social media and 24/7 celebrity coverage, the relationship between celebrities and narcissism has become increasingly complex. Celebrities often serve as cultural touchstones, embodying society's values and desires. However, this heightened visibility can also amplify narcissistic tendencies.

One prominent aspect of celebrity narcissism is the cultivation of a carefully curated public persona. Social media platforms like Instagram and Twitter provide a stage for celebrities to showcase their lives, achievements, and, often, their physical appearances. The constant stream of selfies, lifestyle updates, and endorsements can reinforce narcissistic behaviors, as the pursuit of attention and admiration becomes central to their identity.

Reality television further blurs the line between genuine self-expression and narcissistic self-promotion. Shows like "Keeping Up with the Kardashians" have made fame itself a commodity, with individuals achieving celebrity status for being famous. The concept of being "famous for being famous" underscores the narcissistic undertones of modern celebrity culture.

Furthermore, the relationship between celebrities and their fans has evolved in the digital age. Social media platforms enable direct interactions between stars and their followers, fostering a sense of personal connection. This connection can be empowering, as fans

feel heard and valued, but it can also feed into the narcissistic
tendencies of celebrities who thrive on constant validation and
adoration.

In some cases, celebrity narcissism takes a more destructive turn.
Scandals, public meltdowns, and controversies can be fueled by a
sense of entitlement and an expectation of impunity. The relentless
pursuit of attention and the desire to maintain a perfect image can
lead to risky behavior and unethical choices, with the potential to
harm both the celebrity and their audience.

In conclusion, narcissism in popular culture serves as a reflection
of our society's values and obsessions. Through literature and film,
we explore the complexities of narcissism, from its seductive
allure to its destructive consequences. Meanwhile, the intertwining
relationship between celebrities and narcissism underscores the
evolving nature of fame and self-obsession in the digital age. As
we continue to navigate the intersection of narcissism and popular
culture, it becomes increasingly vital to critically examine the
impact of these representations on our own lives and values.

CHAPTER 11

The Narcissistic Spectrum

- Understanding Degrees of Narcissism

- Overcoming Narcissistic Traits

Narcissism is a term that has become increasingly prevalent in modern psychology and pop culture. It's often used to describe individuals who exhibit self-centered and grandiose behavior, but the reality is far more complex. Narcissism exists on a spectrum, ranging from healthy self-esteem to pathological narcissistic personality disorder (NPD). In this exploration of the narcissistic spectrum, we'll delve into the various degrees of narcissism and discuss strategies for overcoming narcissistic traits.

Understanding Degrees of Narcissism

To comprehend the narcissistic spectrum, it's crucial to recognize that narcissism isn't inherently negative. Healthy narcissism is a normal part of human development and essential for self-esteem and self-worth. However, when narcissistic traits become excessive and rigid, they can lead to significant problems in personal and interpersonal functioning.

1. Healthy Narcissism: At one end of the spectrum lies healthy narcissism. This includes having a positive self-image, self-confidence, and a healthy degree of self-interest. People with healthy narcissism can assert themselves when necessary and maintain a balanced sense of self-worth without demeaning others.

2. Narcissistic Traits: Moving further along the spectrum, we encounter individuals who possess narcissistic traits but don't meet the criteria for narcissistic personality disorder. These traits may include an excessive need for admiration, entitlement, and a lack of empathy. People in this category can be challenging to interact with, as their self-centeredness often overshadows their capacity for empathy and healthy relationships.

3. Narcissistic Personality Disorder (NPD): At the extreme end of the spectrum is Narcissistic Personality Disorder, a diagnosed mental health condition characterized by a pervasive pattern of grandiosity, a constant need for admiration, and a lack of empathy for others. People with NPD often have fragile self-esteem masked by a veneer of superiority, making them highly resistant to criticism.

4. Malignant Narcissism: Beyond NPD, some individuals exhibit what's known as malignant narcissism. This is a combination of narcissistic traits, antisocial behavior, and paranoia. Malignant narcissists can be manipulative, exploitative, and even dangerous to those around them.

Overcoming Narcissistic Traits

Overcoming narcissistic traits, especially when they've become problematic, is a challenging but necessary endeavor for personal growth and healthier relationships. Here are strategies to help individuals move towards the healthier end of the narcissistic spectrum:

1. Self-Reflection: The first step is recognizing that narcissistic traits exist within oneself. Self-awareness is essential for change. Engage in introspection to identify specific behaviors and thought patterns associated with narcissism.

2. Therapy: Seeking professional help, such as psychotherapy, is often crucial for individuals with narcissistic traits. Therapists can provide insight into the underlying causes of narcissism and offer strategies to develop empathy, improve self-esteem, and cultivate healthier relationships.

3. Empathy Development: Practicing empathy is fundamental for reducing narcissistic tendencies. This involves actively listening to others, considering their perspectives, and showing genuine care and concern for their feelings.

4. Self-Esteem Building: Building healthy self-esteem is a key component of overcoming narcissistic traits. This can be achieved through self-compassion, setting realistic goals, and acknowledging personal strengths and weaknesses.

5. Mindfulness and Meditation: Mindfulness practices can help individuals become more self-aware and regulate their emotions. Meditation and mindfulness exercises can also reduce impulsivity and reactivity, common features of narcissistic behavior.

6. Healthy Relationships: Surrounding oneself with supportive and honest individuals can be instrumental in personal growth. Healthy relationships can provide feedback and hold individuals accountable for their behavior.

7. Accepting Criticism: Learning to accept constructive criticism without becoming defensive is essential for personal growth. It can be challenging for those with narcissistic traits, but it's a crucial skill to develop.

8. Setting Boundaries: Establishing and respecting personal boundaries is vital for individuals seeking to overcome narcissistic traits. It ensures healthier interactions and helps manage expectations.

9. Cultivating Humility: Cultivating humility involves recognizing that no one is perfect and that we all make mistakes. Embracing

humility can help counteract the need for constant admiration and validation.

10. Patience and Persistence: Overcoming narcissistic traits is a gradual process that requires patience and persistence. Relapses are common, but each setback can be an opportunity for growth.

In conclusion, understanding the narcissistic spectrum is essential for recognizing that narcissism exists on a continuum from healthy to pathological. Overcoming narcissistic traits involves self-reflection, therapy, empathy development, self-esteem building, mindfulness, and cultivating healthy relationships. While the journey to reducing narcissistic tendencies can be challenging, it is possible and can lead to more fulfilling and meaningful connections with others.

CHAPTER 12

Empathy and Compassion

- Building Empathy

- Coping with Narcissistic Individuals

Empathy and compassion are two fundamental aspects of human interaction that have the power to shape our relationships, influence our actions, and define our sense of self. These qualities are essential for fostering understanding, supporting one another, and building a more compassionate society. In this essay, we will explore the significance of empathy and compassion, their role in building meaningful connections, and how to cope with narcissistic individuals while maintaining these virtues.

Building Empathy

Empathy, often described as the ability to understand and share the feelings of another, is a cornerstone of meaningful human relationships. It's the capacity to step into someone else's shoes, to comprehend their perspective, and to respond with sensitivity and care. Building empathy is a lifelong journey, and here are some key strategies to nurture this essential trait:

1. Active Listening: One of the most effective ways to cultivate empathy is through active listening. When we truly pay attention to what someone is saying, without judgment or interruption, we create a safe space for them to express their thoughts and emotions. This fosters connection and understanding.

2. Perspective-Taking: Try to view situations from another person's perspective. Imagine how they might feel or think in a given situation. This exercise helps break down barriers and promotes empathy.

3. Emotional Awareness: Develop your emotional intelligence by becoming more aware of your own emotions and how they influence your interactions with others. This self-awareness can enhance your ability to empathize with others.

4. Practice Empathetic Responses: Respond to others' emotions with empathy. Show that you understand their feelings and are willing to support them. Simple statements like, "I can imagine that must be tough," or "I'm here for you," can go a long way.

5. Learn from Diverse Perspectives: Engage with people from diverse backgrounds and cultures. Exposure to different viewpoints can broaden your understanding and empathy for people with experiences different from your own.

Coping with Narcissistic Individuals

While empathy and compassion are virtues we should strive to embody, we may encounter narcissistic individuals who pose challenges to maintaining these qualities. Narcissism is characterized by an excessive focus on one's own needs, lack of empathy, and a sense of entitlement. Coping with narcissistic individuals requires a delicate balance of protecting your own well-being while still approaching the situation with empathy and compassion:

1. Set Boundaries: Establish clear boundaries to protect yourself from emotional manipulation or harm. Recognize your limits and communicate them firmly but calmly.

2. Maintain Empathy: While it may be difficult, try to maintain empathy for the narcissistic individual. Understand that their behavior often stems from deep insecurities and wounds. This doesn't excuse their actions but can help you respond with compassion.

3. Self-Care: Prioritize self-care to ensure you are emotionally resilient when dealing with narcissistic individuals. This might involve therapy, meditation, or spending time with supportive friends and family.

4. Seek Support: Reach out to a trusted friend or therapist for support and guidance. Talking to someone can help you process your emotions and navigate complex relationships.

5. Practice Detachment: Learn to detach emotionally from the narcissistic individual's manipulative tactics. Recognize that you cannot change them, but you can control your own responses and actions.

6. Choose Your Battles: Decide when and how to engage with the narcissistic individual. Sometimes, it's best to disengage from pointless arguments and focus on protecting your emotional well-being.

7. Focus on Your Growth: Use your interactions with narcissistic individuals as opportunities for personal growth and self-reflection. Learn from these experiences and become more resilient.

In Conclusion

Empathy and compassion are the threads that weave the fabric of human connection. They are essential for building understanding, nurturing relationships, and promoting a more compassionate world. While building empathy is an ongoing journey that requires self-awareness and practice, coping with narcissistic individuals necessitates setting boundaries, self-care, and maintaining empathy from a distance. By incorporating these principles into our lives, we can contribute to a more empathetic and compassionate society, one relationship at a time.

CHAPTER 13

Self-Care and Boundaries

- Setting Healthy Boundaries

- Self-Care Strategies

Self-care and boundaries are two fundamental aspects of maintaining a healthy and balanced life. In a fast-paced world where the demands of work, relationships, and daily responsibilities can often feel overwhelming, understanding the significance of setting healthy boundaries and implementing self-care strategies is essential for personal well-being. In this exploration of these critical topics, we will delve into the importance of setting boundaries and various self-care strategies that can help individuals lead more fulfilling lives.

Setting Healthy Boundaries

Boundaries are like the invisible fences that define our personal space, both physically and emotionally. They are the limits we establish to protect ourselves from being mistreated, overburdened, or emotionally drained. Setting healthy boundaries is not about building walls; instead, it's about creating a safe and respectful space for oneself.

1. Self-Respect: The foundation of setting boundaries lies in self-respect. When you respect yourself, you recognize your worth and acknowledge that your needs and feelings are just as valid as anyone else's. This self-awareness is crucial in establishing boundaries.

2. Clear Communication: Effective communication is key to setting boundaries. It involves expressing your needs, expectations, and limits to others in a clear and assertive manner. It's important to use "I" statements, such as "I need some alone

time" or "I can't take on any more work right now," to convey your boundaries without blaming or accusing others.

3. Recognizing Warning Signs: Pay attention to situations or relationships where you feel uncomfortable or drained. These are often signs that your boundaries are being violated. Identifying these warning signs can help you take proactive steps to protect your well-being.

4. Consistency: Consistency is vital in maintaining healthy boundaries. If you set a boundary, make sure to stick to it. People may test your boundaries, but by consistently enforcing them, you establish a precedent for respect.

5. Self-Care as a Boundary: Sometimes, setting boundaries means prioritizing self-care. This can include saying no to additional work when you're already overwhelmed, declining social invitations when you need rest, or disconnecting from technology to create space for mental rejuvenation.

6. Adjusting Boundaries: Boundaries are not rigid; they can be adjusted as circumstances change. It's important to be flexible and revisit your boundaries when necessary. Life is dynamic, and what worked in one situation may not work in another.

7. Seeking Support: Seeking support from friends, family, or a therapist can be immensely helpful in establishing and maintaining boundaries. They can provide guidance, validation, and encouragement as you navigate this process.

Self-Care Strategies

Self-care is the deliberate practice of taking time for yourself to recharge, relax, and prioritize your physical, mental, and emotional well-being. It is a vital component of a healthy and balanced life.

1. Prioritizing Sleep: Adequate sleep is the foundation of good health. Ensure you get enough rest each night to rejuvenate your body and mind.

2. Nutrition and Hydration: Eating a balanced diet and staying hydrated provides your body with the essential nutrients it needs to function optimally. Proper nutrition supports both physical and mental well-being.

3. Physical Activity: Regular exercise is not only good for your physical health but also has numerous mental and emotional

benefits. It reduces stress, boosts mood, and increases overall energy levels.

4. Mindfulness and Meditation: These practices help you stay grounded in the present moment, reduce stress, and increase self-awareness. They can be powerful tools for managing anxiety and promoting mental clarity.

5. Hobbies and Interests: Engaging in hobbies and activities you enjoy is a form of self-care. It provides a break from routine and allows you to pursue your passions.

6. Setting Technology Boundaries: In our digital age, it's essential to set boundaries with technology. Designate tech-free times or spaces to disconnect and be fully present in the moment.

7. Social Connection: Maintaining healthy relationships and social connections is an important aspect of self-care. Spending time with loved ones and seeking emotional support when needed can be incredibly beneficial.

8. Professional Boundaries: Just as personal boundaries are crucial, so are professional boundaries. Avoid overworking, set limits on

work-related communication outside of office hours, and take regular breaks to prevent burnout.

9. Seeking Professional Help: When self-care alone isn't enough to manage mental health issues, seeking help from a therapist or counselor is a crucial step toward self-care. They can provide guidance and support tailored to your specific needs.

10. Practice Gratitude: Cultivating a sense of gratitude can shift your perspective and improve your overall well-being. Take time each day to reflect on the things you're thankful for.

In conclusion, self-care and boundaries are integral aspects of maintaining a balanced and fulfilling life. Setting healthy boundaries is an act of self-respect and protection, allowing you to prioritize your well-being. Simultaneously, practicing self-care ensures that you have the physical, mental, and emotional resources to thrive. By embracing these concepts and incorporating them into your daily life, you can cultivate a stronger sense of self, better relationships, and a more satisfying and meaningful existence. Remember, self-care isn't selfish; it's a necessary investment in your overall health and happiness.

CHAPTER 14

Conclusion

- The Journey to Understanding Narcissism

- Promoting Healthy Relationships

In the realm of human psychology and interpersonal dynamics, the concept of narcissism has long been a subject of fascination and concern. This journey of understanding narcissism is a voyage through the intricacies of the human mind, shedding light on its various facets and implications for the formation of healthy relationships. As we conclude this exploration, it's imperative to distill the knowledge gained and emphasize the importance of promoting healthy relationships in a world where narcissism often lurks as a shadow.

Narcissism: Unraveling the Layers

The journey to understanding narcissism begins with delving into its multifaceted nature. Narcissism, as a psychological construct, is characterized by an excessive focus on oneself, a lack of empathy for others, and an inflated sense of self-importance. This personality trait lies on a spectrum, ranging from healthy narcissism, which is a normal part of human development, to pathological narcissism, which can be debilitating and destructive.

We explored the origins of narcissism, tracing it back to early childhood experiences. A child's upbringing, particularly the dynamics within the family, plays a pivotal role in shaping their narcissistic tendencies. Overindulgent or neglectful parenting can contribute to the development of narcissistic traits. Understanding this developmental aspect helps us approach narcissism with empathy, recognizing that it often stems from a place of vulnerability.

The manifestations of narcissism take various forms, with Narcissistic Personality Disorder (NPD) being the extreme end of the spectrum. People with NPD exhibit an insatiable need for admiration, a lack of empathy, and a tendency to exploit others for personal gain. Recognizing these traits is crucial for identifying individuals who may be in need of professional intervention and support.

During our journey, we explored the impact of narcissism on relationships. Narcissists often struggle to maintain healthy, fulfilling connections due to their self-centered tendencies and inability to empathize. This can lead to a cycle of unstable and turbulent relationships, leaving a trail of emotional wreckage in their wake. Understanding the dynamics of narcissistic relationships is essential for those who may find themselves entangled with narcissistic partners, friends, or family members.

Promoting Healthy Relationships: The Antidote to Narcissism

In the face of narcissism's complexities and challenges, promoting healthy relationships becomes a vital countermeasure. Healthy relationships are built on a foundation of mutual respect, empathy, and open communication. They serve as a protective shield against the corrosive effects of narcissism, offering a path to emotional well-being and fulfillment.

One of the key aspects of fostering healthy relationships is setting healthy boundaries. Boundaries act as a buffer against narcissistic behavior, ensuring that individuals can protect their emotional well-being while still engaging in meaningful connections. Learning to say "no" when necessary and clearly communicating one's needs and limits are essential skills in maintaining healthy relationships.

Empathy is the cornerstone of healthy relationships. It's the ability to understand and share the feelings of another person, and it's the antithesis of narcissism. Cultivating empathy is a lifelong journey, but it's one that can transform relationships from shallow interactions to deep, meaningful connections. Empathy enables us to see the humanity in others and fosters genuine understanding.

Effective communication is another vital component of healthy relationships. This involves active listening, expressing oneself honestly and respectfully, and resolving conflicts constructively. By enhancing our communication skills, we can navigate the challenges that arise in any relationship, reducing the likelihood of misunderstandings and hurt feelings.

Self-awareness plays a crucial role in promoting healthy relationships. Understanding our own strengths, weaknesses, and emotional triggers allows us to approach relationships with humility and self-reflection. It also helps us recognize when we might be exhibiting narcissistic tendencies ourselves and take steps to address them.

In our journey to understanding narcissism, we've learned that healthy relationships are not only the antidote but also the aspiration. They provide a template for how we should interact with others, emphasizing mutual respect, empathy, and emotional support. By nurturing healthy relationships, we create an environment where narcissism struggles to thrive.

Conclusion: The Path Forward

In conclusion, the journey to understanding narcissism has been a voyage into the intricacies of human psychology, revealing the many layers of this complex personality trait. From its developmental origins to its impact on relationships, we've explored the multifaceted nature of narcissism.

However, our journey doesn't end with understanding narcissism; it extends to the promotion of healthy relationships as the antidote to narcissistic tendencies. Healthy relationships, characterized by empathy, effective communication, and self-awareness, offer a way forward in a world where narcissism can cast its shadow on our interactions.

As we move forward, let us remember that the path to healthier relationships requires ongoing effort and commitment. It demands that we continually strive to develop our empathy, communication skills, and self-awareness. By doing so, we can not only protect ourselves from the corrosive effects of narcissism but also contribute to a more compassionate and empathetic world where healthy relationships flourish.

CHAPTER 15

Additional Resources

- Books, Articles, and Support Groups

In our quest for knowledge, personal growth, and emotional support, we often find solace and enlightenment in various forms of resources. When it comes to expanding our horizons, seeking expert guidance, or simply connecting with like-minded individuals, books, articles, and support groups play an invaluable role. In this exploration of these additional resources, we will delve into how they can enrich our lives, offer diverse perspectives, and provide essential support.

Books, the timeless companions of the curious mind, are portals to knowledge, imagination, and self-discovery. They offer a unique opportunity to engage with the thoughts and experiences of others, both present and past. The written word transcends time and space, making books a treasure trove of wisdom, ideas, and insights.

The power of books lies not only in their ability to impart information but also in their capacity to evoke empathy and foster understanding. Fiction, for instance, allows readers to step into the shoes of characters from diverse backgrounds, cultures, and eras, thus broadening their worldview. Non-fiction, on the other hand, provides a direct channel to acquire expertise in various fields, from science and history to philosophy and self-help.

One cannot discuss books without mentioning the impact of literature on personal development. Self-help books, such as Dale Carnegie's "How to Win Friends and Influence People" or Viktor E. Frankl's "Man's Search for Meaning," have inspired countless individuals to transform their lives. These books offer practical advice, real-life examples, and philosophical insights that can empower readers to overcome challenges and attain their goals.

Moreover, books serve as a sanctuary for those seeking solace and refuge from the storms of life. Poetry, for instance, offers a unique form of expression that can resonate deeply with one's emotions. Works like Rupi Kaur's "Milk and Honey" or Mary Oliver's "Devotions" have touched the hearts of millions, providing comfort and understanding during difficult times.

While books are a solitary endeavor, articles bridge the gap between traditional print and the fast-paced digital age. The internet has democratized information, making it readily accessible to anyone with a device and an internet connection. This accessibility has given rise to a vast repository of articles covering an array of topics.

Online articles are particularly valuable for staying informed about current events, scientific discoveries, and trends in various industries. Websites like Medium, Forbes, and The New York Times offer a plethora of articles ranging from news to opinion pieces. Readers can choose from a variety of perspectives and sources to gain a well-rounded understanding of a given topic.

Another advantage of articles is their brevity and immediacy. They are perfect for individuals who want to stay updated on the latest developments but have limited time to dedicate to extensive reading. This format allows readers to quickly grasp the main points and decide whether they want to explore a topic further.

Moreover, articles often serve as a bridge between books and support groups. They can introduce readers to new ideas and concepts, sparking an interest that leads them to delve deeper into a subject through books or seek a community of like-minded individuals who share their passions.

Support groups, both online and in-person, provide a unique form of assistance that goes beyond what books and articles can offer. These groups are typically composed of individuals facing similar challenges, whether they be related to health, personal development, or shared interests.

One of the most renowned support group organizations is Alcoholics Anonymous (AA), which has helped countless individuals overcome alcohol addiction through a 12-step program and the support of peers who understand the struggles firsthand. Support groups like AA offer a sense of camaraderie, accountability, and shared wisdom that can be immensely beneficial in the journey to recovery.

Moreover, support groups cater to a wide range of needs. They can focus on mental health, grief counseling, parenting, chronic illness, or hobbies such as gardening or writing. In these gatherings, individuals find solace in knowing they are not alone in their experiences and can learn from others who have walked similar paths.

In recent years, online support groups have gained prominence, thanks to the connectivity of the internet. These digital communities allow individuals from around the world to come together, breaking down geographical barriers. Forums, social media groups, and dedicated websites provide spaces for people to seek advice, share their stories, and offer support.

For example, parenting forums like BabyCenter or Reddit's r/Parenting have become lifelines for new parents, offering a platform to discuss challenges, share tips, and celebrate milestones. Similarly, mental health support groups on platforms like Reddit or Facebook connect people dealing with anxiety, depression, or other conditions, enabling them to seek advice and encouragement from those who understand their struggles.

In conclusion, books, articles, and support groups are indispensable resources that cater to our intellectual, emotional, and communal needs. Books provide a timeless source of knowledge and inspiration, while articles keep us informed and engaged with the world. Support groups offer a unique form of communal support and understanding that can be life-changing for individuals facing various challenges.

The beauty of these resources lies in their versatility and accessibility. Whether you're seeking personal growth, knowledge, or a sense of belonging, books, articles, and support groups are there to guide and support you on your journey through life. In a world where information is abundant, and connection is essential, these additional resources are the compass and companions that can help us navigate the complexities of our existence.